TITHING

GOD'S FINANCIAL PLAN

by

NORMAN ROBERTSON

ORDER FORM

QUANTITY	TITLE	UNIT PRICE	TOTAL
	TWO AUDIO TAPE TEACHING SERIES		
	THE GUIDING VOICE OF THE HOLY SPIRIT	$10.00	
	CHRIST THE HEALER	$10.00	
	FLOWING IN THE ANOINTING	$10.00	
	FINANCIAL INCREASE	$10.00	
	STIRRING UP THE GIFTS OF THE SPIRIT	$10.00	
	HEALING FROM HEAVEN	$10.00	
	MAKING YOUR WAY PROSPEROUS	$10.00	
	KNOWING THE PERSON OF THE HOLY SPIRIT	$10.00	
	LIVING UNDER AN OPEN HEAVEN	$10.00	
	THREE AUDIO TAPE TEACHING SERIES		
	THE HOLY SPIRIT — WHO HE IS AND WHAT HE DOES	$15.00	
	THE MINISTRY OF DIVINE HEALING	$15.00	
	SIX AUDIO TAPE TEACHING SERIES		
	THE SUPERNATURAL CHURCH	$25.00	
	MINISTERING IN THE POWER OF THE HOLY SPIRIT	$25.00	
	BOOKS		
	TITHING—GOD'S FINANCIAL PLAN	$5.00	
	IMPROVING YOUR LOVE LIFE	$5.00	
	WINNERS IN CHRIST	$10.00	
	WORKBOOKS/TRAINING MANUALS		
	THE SUPERNATURAL CHURCH	$15.00	
	MINISTERING IN THE POWER OF THE HOLY SPIRIT	$15.00	
	WALKING IN VICTORY	$15.00	

▼ *SHIPPING & HANDLING COSTS*	SUB-TOTAL	
Up to $30.00 = **$3.00**	ADD SHIPPING & HANDLING COST	
Over $30.00 = **Add 10%**	CONTRIBUTION TO MINISTRY (TAX DEDUCTIBLE)	
All orders must be prepaid SORRY, NO COD's. Please make checks payable to NRM.	TOTAL AMOUNT ENCLOSED $	

Mail Your Order and Payment To:
Norman Robertson Ministries
P.O. Box 3330 ▪ Matthews, NC 28106

OR

Call toll-free:
1-888-NRM-ORDER
All Major Credit Cards Accepted

▼ SHIP TO

Please Print Clearly

Name _____

Address _____

City _____

State _____ Zip _____

_____

Phone _____

☐ **YES**, Brother Norman, your ministry is a blessing and I'd like more information about becoming a partner in ministry with you.

▼ METHOD OF PAYMENT (✓check one)

U.S. Dollars Only

☐ Check ☐ Money Order ☐ Visa
☐ Mastercard ☐ Discover ☐ American Express

Credit Card # _____

Expiration Date _____ Amount charged $ _____

Signature _____

📞 **Phone it:** **1-888-NRM-ORDER**
call toll free

📠 **Fax it:** **1-704-845-9365**

✉️ **Mail it:** **Norman Robertson Ministries**
P.O. Box 3330 • Matthews, NC 28106

CONTENTS

Chapter 1

TITHING PUTS GOD TO THE TEST

*Bring (as an act of worship) the full amount of your tithe
— the whole tenth of your income — into the storehouse
(local church), that there may be food in My house, and
prove Me now by it, go ahead and put Me to the test, check
Me out, experiment with Me, test Me, give Me an opportunity to prove Myself and you will see that I will open the windows of heaven for you — I will throw open the floodgates of
heaven for you — and pour out on you so much blessing
(financially and materially) that you will not have room
enough to contain it.*

*Then I will rebuke the devourer for you — I will protect
the source of your income, I will stop the thief from destroy-
ing the fruit of your labors.*

Malachi 3:10,11 (Paraphrased)

Do you believe the Bible? Do you believe it is God's
Word? Do you believe God gave every promise in the
Bible and that all His promises are true?

If your answer is "yes," and you truly mean that, you

9

will enjoy every word of this book. It will open up to you new channels of blessing and it may even change the entire course of your life. It could bring thousands and even hundreds of thousands of dollars into your bank account. And at the same time, you can build up for yourself an even greater reward to be enjoyed throughout the endless ages of eternity.

THE POWER OF THE TITHE

This is how one man learned that even fearful circumstances can't break God's promise made to those who tithe.

At the age of fourteen, Alexander H. Kerr was converted under the ministry of American evangelist Dwight L. Moody and joined the Presbyterian Church in Philadelphia. In 1902, Mr. Kerr read a book entitled *Judah's Scepter and Joseph's Birthright* by Bishop Allen. In it, Bishop Allen referred to the vow Jacob made in **Genesis 28:22** which says, *"Of all that You give me I will surely give a tenth to You."*

The Scriptures record that twenty years later, Jacob returned to his home with servants and cattle in great abundance. He had become one of the richest men in the East as a result of keeping his covenant of tithing with the Lord.

With some doubts, but with a sincere desire to see whether the Bible is true and whether God's promises are intended for the people of today, on June 1, 1902

Mr. Kerr made a special covenant to set aside the tithe, or ten percent of his income, for the work of the Lord.

At that time, he had a mortgage on his house, owed many obligations, and was burdened with cares and worries — especially of a financial nature. However, he was determined to prove God as Jacob had done. He was challenged by these Scriptures: **Proverbs 3:9-10; Leviticus 27:30-32; Genesis 13:2, 14:20;** and, particularly, **Malachi 3:7-11.**

Mr. Kerr often remarked that if modern day skeptics wanted proof that there is a God, that the Bible is His Holy Word, and that its promises are true, all they needed to do is tithe for one year and God would prove to them, without a doubt, that He is, . . .*the same yesterday, and today, and forever.* . . . (**Hebrews 13:8**).

Within three months of beginning to tithe, unexpected and unforeseen blessings came to Mr. Kerr. It seemed that God had opened his eyes to behold His love and His faithfulness to His promises, especially in regard to tithing. Jesus said in **Matthew 9:29,** *"According to your faith be it unto you."*

That same year Mr. Kerr, with very little capital but with strong faith in God's tithing promises, organized the firm known as Kerr Glass Manufacturing Company. It became one of the largest firms selling fruit jars in the United States.

At the time of the San Francisco earthquake, his fruit jars were being manufactured in the Californian city.

Mr. Kerr had put practically every cent he had into his fruit jar enterprise, and then came the earthquake! His friends came to him and said, "Kerr, you are a ruined man." He replied, "I don't believe it; if I am, then the Bible is not true; I know God will not go back on His promises."

He wired to San Francisco, and received the following reply, "Your factory is in the heart of the fire and undoubtedly is destroyed. The heat is so intense we will be unable to find out anything for some days."

I will rebuke the devourer for your sakes, and he shall not destroy the fruits of your ground.

Malachi 3:11

What a time of testing this was! But Mr. Kerr's faith in the Lord never wavered. He believed **Malachi 3:11** and stood on this promise, unmoved. About a week after the earthquake and fire, a second telegram arrived saying, "Everything for a mile and a half on all sides of the factory burned; but your factory is miraculously saved." God's Word cannot return unto Him void. **(Isaiah 55:8-11.)**

Mr. Kerr immediately boarded a train for San Francisco. The factory was a two-story wooden building containing the huge tanks where the glass was melted. The tanks were kept at a fierce 2500 degrees and oil was used for fuel. The building was probably the most flammable in San Francisco!

The fire had raged on all sides of the factory, creeping up to the wooden fence surrounding the building and even scorching it; then the flames and fire leaped around and over and beyond the building, burning everything in its path. However, not even the wooden fence was burned, nor the building, and not a single glass jar was cracked by earthquake or fire.

This was undoubtedly a display of God's divine power in protecting this man. He held onto his faith that God's promises made to those who tithe would never be broken by any circumstances.

In 1912 Mr. Kerr wrote his first leaflet on the subject of tithing entitled, *God's Cure for Poverty.* This was followed by another tract entitled, *God's Loving Money Rule for Your Financial Prosperity.* Every case of fruit jars that left the factory contained one of these leaflets.

He advertised to give them away to people who would judiciously scatter them — bearing the entire cost himself. From 1912 to the time of his death on February 9, 1924, he had freely distributed more than five million of these leaflets.

Three weeks before his death, he addressed the members of the First Baptist Church of Riverside, California, on the blessings and riches of tithing possessions, income and increase.

Every business in which he had an investment tithed. His returns were so great that he created a *tithing fund* and had it incorporated. His tithing gifts went around the world, for he was deeply interested in the distribution of New Testaments, and Gospel literature.

He rose from poverty to become a millionaire by believing that God would honor His promises and pour out His blessings upon those who accurately and carefully tithe or set aside one-tenth of their possessions, salary or income for the Lord's work.

Do you have a financial fear? Are you afraid to give? I challenge you. Let the Lord give you a release from the fear of financial failure. Put God to the test and see for yourself the supernatural power of tithing!

GOD'S FINANCIAL BLESSINGS

Many have misconceived, unscriptural ideas concerning finances. They believe God wants His people to be poor and destitute. The real truth is that God wants you to prosper financially. He has literally promised to open the windows of heaven and pour you out a blessing (and that means a financial blessing) that you will not have room to contain it!

For many people today, the heavenly windows of God's blessings are closed. Doubt, unbelief, skepticism, or perhaps lack of knowledge of God's Word, have closed them. But though the windows may be closed now, they can be opened for you, if you obey the instructions set forth in this book. The spiritual, physical, and financial blessing of God will be upon you, your household, and everything you set your hands to do as you faithfully honor the Lord in tithes and offerings.

Honor the Lord with your possessions, And with the firstfruits of all your increase;

So your barns will be filled with plenty, And your vats will overflow with new wine.

Proverbs 3:9-10

But seek first the kingdom of God and His righteousness, and all these things shall be added to you.

Matthew 6:33

Consider the testimony of Oswald J. Smith, who was pastor of the People's Church in Toronto, Canada for many years. During the Depression, many people in need came to his office every day to ask for financial help from the church. They gave aid to hundreds of people. He asked all those who came if they had been faithful to tithe when they had an income. In all his experience, no one who came for help had ever been faithful with the tithe. He concluded that God took care of those who had faithfully tithed.

Chapter 2

THE TITHE IS THE LORD'S

And all the tithe of the land, whether of the seed of the land or of the fruit of the tree, is the Lord's. It is holy to the Lord.

Leviticus 27:30

You shall truly tithe all the increase of your grain that the field produces year by year.

Deuteronomy 14:22

And as soon as the commandment was circulated, the children of Israel brought in abundance the firstfruits of grain and wine, oil and honey, and of all the produce of the field; and they brought in abundantly the tithe of everything.

2 Chronicles 31:5

On the first day of the week let each one of you lay something aside, storing up as God has prospered him.

1 Corinthians 16:2

Our money is an essential part of worship. When we give it to God, we are giving an important part of our-

17

selves. We are giving our skills, our talents, our time, and our strength. Our attitude towards money reveals our attitude towards God. We have a choice between God and Mammon. We must serve one or the other.

Tithing is a practical and Scriptural way to put God first with your money. To tithe is to bring the first tenth of your income to God (at your local church) and to have your whole family worship Him with it, and present it to Him. At this time you make a tithing declaration that you are subject to the economy of God and not to the world's economy. You declare with your mouth that depression, inflation, poverty, lack, and debt have no power over you. Tithing is a declaration of your independence from the world's economic system and a declaration of your dependence on the economy of God. When we tithe, we aren't being generous, we are simply obeying God. Therefore, for the Christian, *tithing isn't an option.*

FIRSTFRUITS AND NOT LEFTOVERS

The first of the firstfruits of your land you shall bring into the house of the Lord your God.

Exodus 23:19

Speak to the children of Israel, and say to them: When you come into the land which I give to you, and reap its harvest, then you shall bring a sheaf of the firstfruits of your harvest to the priest.

Leviticus 23:10

All the best of the oil, all the best of the new wine and the grain, their firstfruits which they offer to the Lord, I have given them to you.

Numbers 18:12

That you shall take some of the first of all the produce of the ground, which you shall bring from your land that the Lord your God is giving you, and put it in a basket and go to the place where the Lord your God chooses to make His name abide.

Deuteronomy 26:2

According to these Bible verses, the first thing that should come out of your increase is your tithe. By giving to God first, you actually honor Him with the first-fruits of your increase.

When you give the tithe first, get ready for a pleasant surprise. It will amaze you when you see what God does for the ninety percent you have left. It will go farther than the original one hundred percent would have gone. The reason is that God will rebuke the devourer and remove the curse from your remaining ninety percent.

The Lord wants all the tithe, not everything you have. He doesn't want you to be left empty, His desire is to make you full. He considers your tithe His. It is holy and you should treat it as such.

THE TITHE IS ALWAYS TEN PERCENT

And concerning the tithe of the herd or the flock, or what-

ever passes under the rod, the tenth one shall be holy to the Lord.

Leviticus 27:32

It is easy to prove from God's Word that the tithe is exactly ten percent. We can prove this percentage in two ways. First, the Hebrew and Greek words translated in the Bible as "tithe" literally mean "the tenth." Secondly, we can establish this by comparing two verses of Scripture. They both speak of the same event: Melchizedek's meeting with Abraham.

. . .And he (Abraham) *gave him* (Melchizedek) *a tithe of all.*

Genesis 14:20

Now consider how great this man (Melchizedek) *was, to whom even the patriarch Abraham gave a tenth of the spoils.*

Hebrews 7:4

Notice that in the Genesis account, the word the writer translated as "tithe" is describing the things Abraham gave to Melchizedek. When the Hebrew account uses it, the word "tenth" is speaking of those same things.

It is important to realize the tithe isn't an optional amount of money. It is a specific amount. God's Word plainly states that the tithe is ten percent of all the increase you receive. It would be wrong to say, "I think I'll tithe $35 this month," for the amount of the tithe is unchangeable. It is always ten percent of your increase. When you read what the Scripture actually has to say concerning the percentage amount of the tithe, there is no room left for doubt.

DON'T STEAL GOD'S MONEY

God's Word is very clear about the fact that the person who doesn't tithe is actually stealing from God. God says the non-tither has robbed Him!

Will a man rob God? Yet you have robbed Me! But you say, In what way have we robbed You? In tithes and offerings.

Malachi 3:8

If you aren't tithing, you are taking that which rightfully belongs to God and using it for yourself. Not tithing is a clear violation of God's commandments. In secular terms, not tithing is embezzlement. Not only are you robbing God but you are bringing a curse upon yourself. Please understand that God isn't the One who is cursing you. If you purpose to deny God's provisions and protections, then you curse yourself. That's right, you curse yourself when you don't tithe.

You are cursed with a curse, For you have robbed Me, Even this whole nation.

Malachi 3:9

21

In this verse, Malachi was speaking of the self-imposed penalty (curse) for violating the spiritual principle of tithing. God tells us that there is a penalty for withholding the tithe. Heaven closes over the disobedient. The blessings stop flowing. The many things God wants to do for that person cannot come to pass. If you don't tithe, you don't qualify for the blessings He bestows upon those who do tithe.

TESTIMONY OF ROBERT LAIDLAW

At age eighteen, Robert Laidlaw decided to start giving one-tenth of his income to the Lord. At age twenty, he wrote in his diary, "Before money gets a grip on my heart, by the grace of God I enter into the following pledge with my Lord that:

I will give ten percent of all I earn up to...

If the Lord blesses me with...

I will give fifteen percent of all I earn.

If the Lord blesses me with...

I will give twenty percent of all I earn.

If the Lord blesses me with...

I will give twenty-five percent of all I earn.

The Lord help me to keep this promise for the sake of Christ who gave all for me. Amen!"

At age twenty-five he wrote, "I have decided to change the graduated scale and start giving half — fifty percent — of all my earnings." God so prospered Robert Laidlaw that he became one of the most successful businessmen in New Zealand.

At age seventy he wrote, "I want to bear testimony that, in spiritual communion and in material things, God has blessed me one hundredfold and has graciously entrusted to me a stewardship far beyond my expectations, when as a lad of eighteen, I started to give God a definite portion of my wages."

Chapter 5

TITHING IS FOR TODAY

A church in Kansas needed to replace its treasurer. The elders asked one of their members, the manager of the local grain elevator, to take the job. "I'll do it if you agree to two conditions," he responded.

"What are they?" The church elders asked.

"I'll take the job only if no reports are required for one year, and only if no one asks me any questions for that year."

The man was trusted, respected, honest, and well-known. Though the elders gulped once or twice, they agreed to his terms. They all did business with him since he managed the only grain elevator for miles around.

At the end of the year, the treasurer gave his report to the congregation. The debt of the church building had been paid in full. The salaries of the staff had been increased substantially. A new van had been purchased and paid in full. All missions commitments had been met. There were no outstanding bills to be paid and there was a surplus of several thousand dollars.

The shocked congregation immediately asked the obvious question, "How could this be?"

"It's simple," the treasurer replied. "Most of you bring your grain to my elevator. As you did business with me during the year, I withheld ten percent on your behalf and gave it to the church in your name. You never missed it. Do you see what we could do for the church and the Lord's work if we continued to give Him the first tenth?"

Tithing isn't something you do because you can afford to do it. It is something you do to honor God. It is an act of obedience, trust, faith, and confidence in Him. Why is this important? It is important because giving your tithes into the good ground of your local church is necessary to keep the windows of heaven open over your finances.

Bring all the tithes into the storehouse, That there may be food in My house, And prove Me now in this, Says the Lord of hosts, If I will not open for you the windows of heaven....
Malachi 3:10

You can't expect to reap financial miracles unless the windows of heaven are open over your life. Not tithing invites Satan into your life. He is the adversary whom the Bible calls "the devourer." Scripture shows there is only one way to stop the devourer immediately and that is to start tithing regularly.

WHY IS TITHING FOR TODAY?

Some believers say tithing falls under the Old Testament Mosaic Law. Therefore, because Christians are living under grace in the New Testament, tithing doesn't apply to them today. But tithing is an eternal principle of God's Word. According to the Bible, the practice of tithing came over four hundred years **before the Mosaic Law** was given.

Then Melchizedek king of Salem brought out bread and wine; he was the priest of God Most High,

And he blessed him and said: Blessed be Abram of God Most High, Possessor of heaven and earth;

And blessed be God Most High, Who has delivered your enemies into your hand.

And he gave him a tithe of all.

Genesis 14:18-20

In this account, Abram had just won a tremendous war against several kings and the spoils of that war were vast. On his way home from the final battle, he met Melchizedek, who was a priest and king unto God. When Melchizedek reminded Abram that it was God who gave him the great victory and wealth, his heart was filled with thanksgiving. He immediately gave Melchizedek a tenth of everything to honor the Lord. This was about 430 years before the law of Moses.

Later, his grandson Jacob tithed to the Lord. He did this 270 years before the Mosaic Law.

Then Jacob made a vow, saying, If God will be with me, and keep me in this way that I am going, and give me bread to eat and clothing to put on,

So that I come back to my father's house in peace, then the Lord shall be my God.

And this stone which I have set as a pillar shall be God's house, and of all that You give me I will surely give a tenth to You.

Genesis 28:20-22

In the New Testament Jesus Himself confirmed the practice of tithing.

Woe to you, scribes and Pharisees, hypocrites! For you pay tithe of mint and anise and cummin, and have neglected the weightier matters of the law: justice and mercy and faith. These you ought to have done, without leaving the others undone.

Matthew 23:23

But woe to you Pharisees! For you tithe mint and rue and all manner of herbs, and pass by justice and the love of God. These you ought to have done, without leaving the others undone.

Luke 11:42

In the Book of Hebrews, tithing is connected with the eternal and unchanging priesthood of Melchizedek **(Hebrews 7:1-8)**, proving again that it is a New Testament principle.

Here mortal men receive tithes, but there He (Jesus) *receives them of whom it is witnessed that He lives.*

Hebrews 7:8

We must realize that tithing didn't begin or end with the Mosaic Law, but is a fundamental principle of God's Word and applies to all believers in all times.

TITHING IS A NEW TESTAMENT PRINCIPLE

You will find very little mention of the tithe in the New Testament. The reason is simple. The tithe was such a well established principle, the people were so thoroughly instructed as to its necessity, importance, and blessing that it wasn't necessary to reinforce this teaching in the New Testament. Jesus placed His approval upon it. Isn't that enough?

Colossians 2:14 tells us that Jesus blotted out the Mosaic Law by nailing it to His cross. But this doesn't affect the tithe, which was in place before the law. Paul, in **1 Corinthians 9:6-14** confirmed the continued use of tithes and offerings as a means of supporting the ministry and the work of the Lord:

Or is it only Barnabas and I who have no right to refrain from working? Who ever goes to war at his own expense? Who plants a vineyard and does not eat of its fruit? Or who tends a flock and does not drink of the milk of the flock?

Do I say these things as a mere man? Or does not the law say the same also? For it is written in the law of Moses, You shall not muzzle an ox while it treads out the grain. Is it oxen God is concerned about?

Or does He say it altogether for our sakes? For our sakes, no doubt, this is written, that he who plows should plow in hope, and he who threshes in hope should be partaker of his hope.

If we have sown spiritual things for you, is it a great thing if we reap your material things? If others are partakers of this right over you, are we not even more? Nevertheless we have not used this right, but endure all things lest we hinder the gospel of Christ.

Do you not know that those who minister the holy things eat of the things of the temple, and those who serve at the altar partake of the offerings of the altar?

Even so the Lord has commanded that those who preach the gospel should live from the gospel.

In the Old Testament, Moses said,

And all the tithe of the land, whether of the seed of the land or of the fruit of the tree, is the Lord's. It is holy to the Lord.

Leviticus 27:30

Nothing could be clearer. The tithe is the Lord's ! It was the Lord's in 1491 B.C., and is still His today in 1994 A.D. Nowhere in the Bible has God declared that the tithe was no longer to be His.

Everything we have comes from God and belongs to Him. **Psalm 50:10** says *And the cattle on a thousand hills belong to God.* **Haggai 2:8** says, *The silver is Mine, and the gold is Mine.* . . . When we raise a crop, God gives the soil (**Psalm 24:1**), the seed (**Genesis 1:11**), and the rain (**Job 5:10**).

In addition, you couldn't do your part if God didn't give you life (**Acts 17:28**) and health (**Jeremiah 30:17**), and strength (**Psalm 144:1**).

God can get along without your tithe, but you can't get along without giving it. God can get along without you, but you can't get along without Him.

WHERE SHOULD THE TITHE BE GIVEN?

There is much confusion as to where the tithe should be given. Some say it should go to the local church. Others say Bible colleges should receive it. Still others want the tithe to go strictly for world evangelism, or else into the television ministries.

What I understand to be the Biblical answer is found in Malachi chapter 3. It says that the tithe should go into "the storehouse." The context indicates that this storehouse is the place where the "meat" — the Word of God — is kept and supplied to God's people. The

31

storehouse and God's house are one and the same.

In Old Testament Israel, the storehouse was the tabernacle and then became the temple. Today, it is your local church. You should attend an anointed local church and faithfully bring your tithes into that ministry. Timothy gives us New Testament clarity on this subject by identifying the local church as the house of God. It is the place where the Word of God is stored.

Know how you ought to conduct yourself in the house of God, which is the church of the living God. . . .

1 Timothy 3:15

Where should you tithe? You should give your tithe to the place where you and your family worship the Lord. It is in your local church that you and your family receive spiritual food, help, and strength. Every Christian needs to find a Bible-believing, Holy Ghost filled church in order to fulfill their responsibility to the work of God in their community through supporting the ministries of their church.

Without finances in the house of God, the Gospel can't be preached and taught. Yes, the Gospel is free but it takes money to get it out to the world and to feed the sheep. The money we give makes it possible to preach and teach the Word of God so that people can come and be born again, healed, delivered from Satan's power, and receive spiritual nourishment from the Word.

The Bible doesn't tell you to use the tithe to purchase Christian tapes and books. That is purchasing, not tithing. The Bible doesn't tell you to use the tithe to pay for your Bible school tuition and fees. That is payment, not tithing. The Bible doesn't tell you to divide the tithe into portions and give two percent to your local church, three percent to your favorite evangelist, two percent to the Salvation Army, two percent to buy groceries for poor sister Mary, and one percent to the "Cat and Dog Society." You are to bring the entire tithe into the storehouse.

Where are you being fed God's Word? Where do you fellowship with other believers and receive help and Godly counsel? Where do you submit yourself to leadership and receive guidance and direction? This is your local church and this is where your tithe belongs.

When you eat at a restaurant, you don't pay your bill at a different restaurant down the street. You can't eat at a five-star restaurant and pay the bill at the local burger house. In the same way, God tells us to bring the whole tenth into the storehouse.

DON'T GIVE YOUR TITHE TO A DEAD CHURCH

The Bible that teaches us where to tithe also teaches us where *not* to tithe.

I have not eaten of the tithe in my mourning (making the tithe unclean), nor have I handled any of it when I was unclean, nor given any of it to the dead; I have hearkened to

*the voice of the Lord my God, and have done according to
all that You have commanded me.*

Deuteronomy 26:14 (AMP)

Don't give your tithes to a dead ministry or a religious graveyard. By this I mean a "passed away" church.
Those religious churches teach that healing has passed
away, tongues have passed away, and miracles have
passed away. In this kind of church, you may not even
be taught that you must be born again and the Bible
may not be considered the inerrant Word of God.

In this kind of church, no one is getting saved,
healed, or delivered. No one is coming to an intimate
relationship with the Father through Jesus Christ. And
when you tithe to a church that rejects miracles, waters
down or alters the Gospel, and can't help people come
to God and change their lives for the better, your tithe
is giving approval to a dead work.

Don't put your stamp of approval on dead churches!

The Bible specifically says that we arc not to tithc to
the dead! If the church you attend is spiritually dead,
and you are giving your tithes and offerings to that
church, then you are actually giving to the dead.

How can you tell if you are in a dead church? If the
life of God is in a church, people will be getting saved,
healed, and delivered. People will grow spiritually and
become more responsible and stable in their lives.
When the life of God is in a place, there is Holy Spirit
power and people will be changed and transformed to
become more like Jesus.

One preacher visited a church overseas and said, "The only thing moving in this church is the ivy growing up the side of the wall!" Don't give the Lord's money to such a place. You have no right to put God's money in a graveyard. It is your responsibility to tithe where God's uncompromised Word is ministered, where your needs are met, and where you and your family receive spiritual nutrition. Become a partner in a local church that is continually winning souls and getting people filled with the Holy Spirit, healing the sick, and teaching our heritage in Jesus Christ.

THE "BEATITUDES" OF TITHING

✓ *Blessed* are the tithers, for they are obeying one of God's fundamental laws.

✓ *Blessed* are the tithers, for they are partners with God.

✓ *Blessed* are the tithers, for they are helping to extend the kingdom of God and establish His covenant on the earth.

✓ *Blessed* are the tithers, for they aren't guilty of robbing God.

✓ *Blessed* are the tithers, for the windows of heaven will open to pour out upon them financial and material blessings.

✓ *Blessed* are the tithers, for they are the ones who become cheerful givers, beloved of God.

✓ *Blessed* are the tithers, for they have divine protection from Satan and the devourer cannot touch their finances.

Chapter 4

TITHING IS WORSHIP

Bring all the tithes into the storehouse, That there may be food in My house, And prove Me now in this, Says the Lord of hosts,

If I will not open for you the windows of heaven And pour out for you such blessing That there will not be room enough to receive it.

Malachi 3:10

"Low Investment — High Return at No Risk!" was the headline carried in the advertising section of a financial newspaper. This is what tithing is all about! Tithing is God's way of financing His kingdom on the earth. It is His system of economics which enables the Gospel to be preached and people to be saved, healed, and delivered. Specifically, tithing underwrites and supports the ministry costs of the local church. It was never God's plan for His work to be financed by having bake sales, garage sales, or car washes.

When you tithe in obedience to God's Word, you are placed in a position to be blessed financially. It places you in a position to receive prosperity and financial security from God, even in difficult economic times.

In the Old and New Testaments, the Hebrew and Greek words for "tithe" mean exactly the same thing: a tenth. When you tithe to the Lord, you give a tenth of your earnings to your local church. The Bible teaches that the tithe belongs to God.

And all the tithe of the land, whether of the seed of the land or of the fruit of the tree, is the Lord's. It is holy to the Lord.

And concerning the tithe of the herd or the flock, of whatever passes under the rod, the tenth one shall be holy to the Lord.

Leviticus 27:30,32

The tithe is God's property, not ours. This means that tithing is not optional. Ten percent of your salary, profit in your business, profit from investments, and any financial gift belongs to God. It is just as holy unto the Lord as water baptism or communion.

YOUR MONEY CAN BE SPIRITUAL

Deuteronomy 26:1-12 states that giving tithes and offerings are specific worship services before God. Satan has lied to the Body of Christ and has somehow convinced us that money is evil or at least unspiritual. That's a lie! Money is a spiritual matter. It is one of the acceptable Scriptural offerings for the worship of the

Lord. Money is an effective tool to help bring the message of salvation to lost souls throughout the world. When you put your money into use according to Biblical principles and with a truly Scriptural heart, your finances become a sacred matter.

Money is your life. Each week when you are paid, the paycheck you receive is the company's way of reimbursing you for the time you spend in service to them. It is a mistake to think of money as something dirty or unworthy because money is part of us. When we offer it, we are offering a major part of ourselves to God.

God told Israel that no one should appear before Him empty-handed. The psalmist said, *Bring an offering and come into God's courts and worship Him in the beauty of holiness.* (**Psalm 96:8,9.**) Bringing an offering is essential to access God and to offer Him true worship.

In too many of our churches, there is no worship of God and no faith exercised when the tithes and offerings are received. The pastor and the people alike look upon the offering as a burden and not a blessing. The preacher apologizes for taking the offering, assuring the people that he wishes it weren't necessary and that if it were possible, he would preach the Gospel without money. This religious attitude about money has allowed Satan to keep the church poor and in lack for years.

WHO REALLY GETS MY MONEY?

Many people wonder, "I know that the church uses

my tithe to meet the salaries of the pastor and the staff, for the maintenance of the building, and to help those in need. But why do we say we are giving our money to God?"

In **1 Corinthians 10:11,** the Holy Spirit tells us that everything written about the children of Israel in the Old Testament is for our education and benefit. We are to look to the Old Testament types and shadows as examples for the Church today.

In **Deuteronomy 26**, details about tithing give insight into worshiping the Lord with our tithe. These were God's instructions to the nation of Israel. If we continue reading the passage from Deuteronomy, we can see how we are to respond to the great prosperity into which God has brought us.

That you shall take some of the first of all the produce of the ground, which you shall bring from your land that the Lord your God is giving you, and put it in a basket and go to the place where the Lord your God chooses to make His name abide.

And you shall go to the one who is priest in those days, and say to him, I declare today to the Lord your God that I have come to the country which the Lord swore to our fathers to give us.

Then the priest shall take the basket out of your hand and set it down before the altar of the Lord your God.

Deuteronomy 26:2-4

We are to take the firstfruits, not the leftovers, of our income and present them to the priest, worshiping the Lord with the abundance He has given us.

Honor the Lord with your possessions, and with the firstfruits of all your increase;

So your barns will be filled with plenty, And your vats will overflow with new wine.

Proverbs 3:9,10

Who is our priest today? The Lord Jesus Christ is! It is Jesus Himself Who receives our tithes and offerings.

Therefore, holy brethren, partakers of the heavenly calling, consider the Apostle and High Priest of our confession, Christ Jesus.

Hebrews 3:1

Seeing then that we have a great High Priest who has passed through the heavens, Jesus the Son of God, let us hold fast our confession.

Hebrews 4:14

Here mortal men (God's ministers on earth) *receive tithes, but there He* (Jesus Christ in Heaven) *receives them, of whom it is witnessed that He lives.*

Hebrews 7:8

Deuteronomy 26:4 tells us that Jesus receives our tithes personally and places them before the altar of God. Can you see where we have missed it by just stuffing some money into an envelope and dropping it into the offering basket without a thought and without worship?

Jesus Himself then directs the pastor concerning the distribution of the tithes and offerings. Therefore, when we give tithes and offerings, we can truly say we are giving to the Lord.

And you shall answer and say before the Lord your God: My father was a Syrian, about to perish, and he went down to Egypt and sojourned there, few in number; and there he became a nation, great, mighty and populous.

But the Egyptians mistreated us, afflicted us, and laid hard bondage on us.

Then we cried out to the Lord God of our fathers, and the Lord heard our voice and looked on our affliction and our labor and our oppression.

So the Lord brought us out of Egypt with a mighty hand and with an outstretched arm, with great terror and with signs and wonders.

He has brought us to this place and has given us this land, a land flowing with milk and honey.

And now, behold, I have brought the firstfruits of the land which You, O Lord, have given me.

Then you shall set it before the Lord your God, and worship before the Lord your God.

Deuteronomy 26:5-10

In this passage of Scripture, the Holy Spirit reveals to Israel the confession they are to declare as they present their tithes and offerings. They are to rehearse their great deliverance from Egypt and proclaim the grace and mercy of God that redeemed them from bondage.

Likewise, under the new covenant (**Colossians 1:13,14, Psalm 107:2),** we are to confess our redemption through the shed Blood of Jesus Christ when we bring our tithes before Him.

THE BELIEVER'S TITHE DECLARATION

Let the redeemed of the Lord say so, Whom He has redeemed from the hand of the enemy.

Psalm 107:2

Based upon **Deuteronomy 26,** this prayer declaration is to be prayed over your tithes as you worship the Lord in your giving.

"Father God, in the Name of Jesus I confess this day that I have come into the inheritance which You promised to give me. I have come into the land which You provided for me through Jesus Christ, the kingdom of Almighty God. I was a sinner serving Satan but I called upon the Name of Jesus Christ and You heard my cry and delivered me from the power and authority of darkness. You translated me into the kingdom of Your dear Son.

"Jesus, as my Lord and High Priest, I bring the firstfruits

43

of my income to You and worship the Lord God with it. I rejoice in all the good which You have given to me and my household. I have obeyed Your voice and have done according to all that You have commanded me.

"Father God, in Jesus' Name, look down from Your holy habitation and bless me as You promised in Your Word. By faith I know that You have opened the windows of heaven above me and are pouring out on me Your abundant blessings!

"Lord, I thank You that the devourer has been rebuked and Satan rendered helpless in my finances. I praise and thank You for the privilege and benefits of tithing. This is my confession of faith in Jesus' Name. Amen."

Chapter 5

TITHING OPENS THE WINDOWS OF HEAVEN

Present as an act of worship the full tithe — the whole tenth of your income, bringing it into the storehouse so that there can be meat in My house and prove Me now by it, go ahead and put Me to the test, try Me, check Me out, experiment with Me, give Me an opportunity to prove Myself, I challenge you to challenge Me and you will see that I will open the windows of heaven for you — I will release the flood gates of heaven and pour out upon you financial and material blessings until you overflow with abundance.

Then I will rebuke the devourer for you — I will protect the source of your income — I will stop the thief stealing from you and he will not destroy the fruit of your righteous labors and you will not fail to receive a fruitful harvest says the Lord your God.

Malachi 3:10,11 (Hebrew Translation)

The windows of heaven are opened by the faithful giving of tithes, making this basic giving absolutely necessary. Nothing can flow from God to you or me if those windows aren't open.

By digging into God's Word you will discover that the phrase "windows of heaven" actually means "floodgates." It is the same word used in **Genesis 7:11** where God opened the windows of heaven and flooded the earth with water. God doesn't use empty figures of speech. He means what He says! He will open the floodgates of heaven and pour out an abundant blessing on the tither.

. . . And prove Me now in this. . . If I will not open for you the windows of heaven. . . .

Malachi 3:10

Tithing is the first step towards living under an open heaven, for God promises to open the windows of heaven over the tither. Because of this promise we know the opposite is also true. Failing to tithe will close those windows. Failing to tithe brings a curse upon your finances!

Withholding God's tithes and offerings places you outside of His will and outside of His blessings and protection. The curse means that you won't be blessed as you come in or as you go out. There will be no blessing upon that which you set your hands to do or upon the fruit of your ground, your cattle, your flocks, or your herds. There will be no blessing upon your basket nor your store and your barns won't be filled, but remain empty. God's good treasure won't be opened unto you, neither will the windows of heaven. They will be closed and locked! Hoping to become plenteous in goods, so that there will be sufficient to meet your own needs with some left over, you will instead find that you must borrow rather than lend. Instead of being blessed, you will be cursed. When you rob God, you are actually robbing yourself by giving Satan legal access to attack you with the curse of lack.

EXPERIMENTING WITH GOD

The late Perry Hayden performed an experiment that was publicized throughout the United States. He wanted to prove that the law of the tithe was the divine law of prosperity. So he decided to plant one cubic inch of wheat and each year, tithe the increase. Perry Hayden planted the first crop in 1940 and then planted the increase, minus the tithe, the following year.

Henry Ford soon became interested in the experiment and furnished the land and equipment for harvesting the crop. But I will let Mr. Hayden tell the story for it shows the remarkable results possible in a wheat yield when the blessing of God is upon it:

"On Sunday morning, 22 September, 1940, I heard a message preached on **John 12:24**, *Verily, verily, I say unto you, Except a corn of wheat fall into the ground and die, it abideth alone: but if it die, it bringeth forth much fruit.*

"Being a miller and being interested in actually proving God in a rather unique way, I was led to do something the following Thursday that has since been heard of all the way around the world. I planted 360 kernels of wheat (one cubic inch). It takes 2,150 cubic inches to make a bushel, so you can see what a small beginning this was.

"When we planted the wheat, 26 September, 1940, on a plot four by eight feet, I told those present that in 1941 we were going to tithe the crop and replant it. I was taking **Malachi 3:10** seriously.

"In **Leviticus 25:3,4** we find the Bible says to 'sow the field' for six years and let it rest the seventh. That is what we set out to do.

"In 1941 we cut the 'world's smallest wheat field.' Immediately, we turned over a tenth of the yield to the local Quaker church and replanted the remaining 45 cubic inches in September of 1941.

"In the summer of 1942, we cut the second crop with old-fashioned cradles and found the yield was fifty-five fold, or 70 pounds. Again we tithed the wheat and replanted the remaining 63 pounds on land that, for the third year in succession, had been furnished by Henry Ford, who owned a large farm near Tecumseh.

"In 1943, this acre of land yielded 16 bushels from the one bushel of seed. Henry Ford himself came out to see the wheat cut, and furnished a reaper to cut it and an old-fashioned thresher from his famous Edison

Institute Museum at Greenfield Village, to thresh it.

"Not only that, but Henry again furnished land for the fourth crop. In 1944, this crop on 14 acres yielded 380 bushels.

"Again, the tenth of the crop was tithed and the remaining cleaned and replanted. Henry Ford furnished land for the fifth crop. It was 230 acres. In the summer of 1945 a fleet of 40 combines was sent to the field by Ford. The yield from the dynamic kernels was 5,555 bushels. The value of this little crop at the market price of $1.55 per bushel, was $8,610.25.

"The tithe of $861.03 went to the Friends Church who, in turn, gave it to the Tecumseh Hospital.

"And now comes the interesting outcome after Henry Ford had turned over the fifth crop to me. The 5,000 bushels of wheat were sold to approximately 250 farmers in Michigan and nearby states. They had to agree to plant the wheat, and in 1946, to pay a tithe of their crop to their local church. In the summer of 1946 we expected to harvest $100,000 worth of wheat — all from 360 kernels planted six years before, which for five years had been faithfully tithed.

"Mr. Henry Ford's assistance in furnishing land, machines, and labor for the first five years was deeply appreciated. And it was all voluntary on his part. How thrilled I was on different occasions when he might visit the wheat field at Tecumseh, or when I might visit him at Dearborn, to hear him say, 'You had faith, didn't you!' or 'You are being led, aren't you?'

"The very last words Mr. Ford said to me one day after he had visited for possibly an hour were, 'God is within you!' "

THE BENEFITS OF HONORING THE LORD

Honoring God with the tenth — obeying the principle of the tithe — will put you in a legal position to receive the blessings of God. However, if you don't tithe, you place yourself under a financial curse and in a position to be attacked by the devil.

The good news for every child of God is that when you tithe, **you are taking dominion** in the financial realm. You have the right to receive what is promised in **Malachi 3,** and you are in a position to be legally free from Satan's bondage.

Perhaps you are one of the many people who think tithing was only for the Old Testament and has no value today. If you are, I encourage you to study the following Scriptural benefits, they will encourage you to become a steady worshiper of God with your tithes.

BENEFIT NUMBER 1

There will be spiritual nourishment, "meat," in the

local church to feed God's people. Tithing is God's financial system of maintaining His Church.

God's Word in Malachi talks about "meat in My house" (local church).

God's Word is likened to:

> Bread **(Luke 4:4)**
>
> Milk **(1 Peter 2:2)**
>
> Meat **(Hebrews 5:14)**

The tithe supports God's ministry so that God's ministers, pastors, and teachers can feed the flock of God with the meat of His Word.

If God's ministers aren't well supported financially and forced to work at secular employment, they will be unable to spend their time in the Word and in prayer in preparation to serve their flock a "nourishing, appetizing, spiritual menu." Instead, they will be feeding their congregations "dry crusts and stale bread." The sheep will be cheated and starved.

When there is a lack of sufficient finances to support the ministry of the local church, the lack of meat will result in a lack in your life. Lack of meat causes a lack of the Word going forth, and therefore a lack of spiritual nourishment.

One Hebrew scholar states that a rendering of the word "storehouse" is "ammunition storage place." In other words, it is the place where believers come and get equipped, charged up, and sent forth as overcomers to pull down Satan's strongholds. As God's ministers, it is our responsibility to feed and equip God's people with the meat of the Word! **(Acts 6:4.)**

The meat of the Word isn't a watered down religious Gospel but the non-compromising Word of life that is taught in the power and demonstration of the Holy Spirit. The meat of the Word is the "full gospel" message, not half a gospel or twenty percent gospel!

BENEFIT NUMBER 2

God's blessing will be released, causing abundant financial prosperity. Tithing releases the floodgates of heaven's blessings upon you just like the flood in Noah's day.

As stated before, the phrase "windows of heaven" in the Hebrew actually means "floodgates." It is the same word used in **Genesis 7:11** where the earth was flooded and there wasn't enough room to receive all that water. The way God opened the floodgates of heaven to flood the whole earth is the same way He will open the floodgates of heaven to bless you.

When we tithe, the hands of the devourer and thief — the devil — are bound. Satan is unable to come in and steal, kill, or destroy our finances or goods. (John 10:10.) God's promise to the tither is insurance against Satan. It is your personal income protection. Relative to the tithe, God says He will rebuke the devourer for your sake.

BENEFIT NUMBER 3

God's rebuke goes into action and provides financial protection. When you begin tithing and start claiming your benefits, God guarantees to protect the source of your income and block negative financial results from affecting your life.

By standing on the Word of God we can defeat the devourer's attacks on our finances by saying, "My God has promised to open the flood gates of heaven and pour out a greater blessing than I can receive. Satan, you are rebuked in Jesus' Name!" Child of God, tithing is your **personal income protection policy** according to **Malachi 3:11**.

BENEFIT NUMBER 4

You are tapping into God's divine source of supply and placing yourself in a legal position to be abundantly supplied, according to the living conditions of heaven and not according to the living conditions of this earth.

BENEFIT NUMBER 5

Tithing supersedes natural laws and releases God's laws of increase and multiplication to become manifest in your life.

BENEFIT NUMBER 6

The tithe protects the remaining ninety percent of

your income and multiplies it. If you don't tithe, you are denying God the portion that rightfully belongs to Him and opening the door to be attacked by Satan.

BENEFIT NUMBER 7

As a tither, you can expect to have favor with God and man. Expect God's divine favor to multiply your sales, to bring you promotion, and to increase your income.

BENEFIT NUMBER 8

As a tither, when you give to God's kingdom, He will give you creative, inspired ideas. The Holy Spirit will give you wisdom and guidance in your career, showing you better ways of doing things. He will send you the right customers, the right clients, the best contracts, and the best deals.

Pray this: "God, give me an inspired idea that will bless this world and prosper me financially to advance your kingdom and establish your covenant on the earth."

Businesses today need fresh ideas and new concepts. God will show you solutions that will put you over and make your way prosperous.

BENEFIT NUMBER 9

You are exercising dominion in the area of your finances. You are lifting yourself out of the curse of financial bondage and you are reversing the curse with blessing!

BENEFIT NUMBER 10

Tithing binds the hands of the enemy from stealing your money. You put handcuffs on the devil and spoil his works.

TITHING REALLY WORKS

Upon receiving Jesus Christ into his life, a Johannesburg businessman immediately questioned the teaching he had been receiving on tithes and offerings. He related the following testimony:

"**Malachi 3:8-11** was shown to me and I decided to act on it. Just over a year later I attended Rhema Bible Training Center in Johannesburg to establish my life in God's Word. But through a series of negative situations, halfway through the year my business took a turn for the worse. I ended up in tremendous debt and became very discouraged. As a result, I left the school.

"Two weeks later, the Lord showed me that I should continue my studies. **Job 36:11** says, *If they obey and serve Him, They shall spend their days in prosperity, And their years in pleasures.* So I decided, 'You must obey God when He directs and speaks to you.'

"During that time, we had a dynamic teaching seminar on God's laws of giving and receiving by Pastor

Norman Robertson. It made me realize that I had not sown correctly, and I was not claiming what was rightfully mine as a tither! I saw I had to claim prosperity in the same way I accepted and received physical healing.

> *Thus says the Lord your Redeemer, the Holy One of Israel: I am the Lord your God, Who teaches you to profit, Who leads you by the way you should go.*
>
> *Isaiah 48:17*

"At that point, I made a decision to implement what I had been taught by Pastor Robertson. So I began sowing correctly (**Malachi 3:8-12** and **2 Corinthians 9:6-10**) and claiming my tithing benefits, plus a hundredfold return from my offerings.

"Within three months, I was totally out of debt, and had money in the bank. This was an incredible turnaround of $200,000 in three months. I must mention at this point that my company only netted approximately that much in the previous calendar year.

"I believe that there was a supernatural move by God in those three months, because I trusted God's Word on tithing and acted upon it. I can clearly see His hand of blessing and protection on my business. What God has done for me I know He will do for you!"

When believers tithe, knowing and acting on their tithing rights, they will prosper financially because they are, in fact, activating their covenant with God.

Chapter **6**

THE HONEST TRUTH ABOUT TITHING

And you shall know the truth, and the truth shall make you free.

John 8:32

My beloved children it is my desire above everything else that you prosper in life, succeed in business, enjoy good health and be diligent about prospering your soul.

3 John 2 (Strong's Translation)

God's Word lays out specific conditions and principles for a life of abundant prosperity. If we will diligently apply them, those principles will cause us to receive the blessings He wants us to have.

God prospers us because He is a loving Father who provides good things for His children. He prospers us because He has made specific covenant promises to us. **(Malachi 3:10,11, Luke 6:38, 2 Corinthians 9:6-10.)** God prospers us so that we can use our financial blessing to be a blessing and financial channel for His work. **(Deuteronomy 8:18)**

ARE YOU TIPPING INSTEAD OF TITHING?

The April 1988 issue of *Christian Retailing* carried an article by Ralph Rath which revealed that the average charismatic Christian spends only $2.17 per week on all Christian related items. That isn't just tithes and offerings but represents what he or she spends on all Christian causes.

Let this sink in! American Christians spend thirty-four percent of their wages to pay Caesar (the government), while they spend less than two percent on all Christian endeavors combined. This leaves God with nothing more than a tip!

God wants your first and your best. This isn't greedy when you consider that everything on the earth is the Lord's. **(Psalm 24:1.)** As a Christian, everything about you and all that is yours belongs to Him. Aren't you glad the Lord said to give Him ten percent and keep ninety percent to live on, rather than give Him ninety percent and live on ten percent?

SCRIPTURAL TRUTHS ABOUT TITHING

Study the checklist below. It will help remind you of the basic truths on tithing. You may want to copy it and place it in your Bible to refer to from time to time.

NUMBER 1

Tithing is God's way of financing His kingdom on the earth so that the Gospel can go forth and people can be saved, healed, delivered, and set free from Satan. Tithing, not things like cake and bake sales, garage sales, car washes, or selling t-shirts, underwrites the ministry costs of the local church.

NUMBER 2

The Bible teaches that the word "tithe" means to give the tenth portion. Ten percent of all your income belongs to the Lord. One-tenth of everything you receive — salary, business profits, profits from your investments, financial gifts — rightfully belongs to God. **(Leviticus 27:30.)**

NUMBER 3

The Bible teaches that the tithe is holy unto the Lord and is a sacred ordinance just like holy communion. **(Leviticus 27:32, Malachi 3:7, Deuteronomy 26:13.)** Therefore, for the believer to misuse or spend God's tithe is to make unclean that which is holy before Him.

NUMBER 4

Tithing was instituted and practiced before the law. Abram tithed to Melchizedek 430 years prior to the law of Moses. **(Genesis 14:18-20.)**

NUMBER 5

Tithing was incorporated into the law of Moses and was a regular practice during the dispensation of the law. **(Leviticus 27, Deuteronomy 26.)**

NUMBER 6

The Lord Jesus Christ Himself was a tither and He confirmed the practice of tithing in the New Testament. **(Matthew 23:23, Luke 11:42.)**

NUMBER 7

Hebrews 7:1-8 is further proof that tithing is for today and should be practiced by every New Testament believer.

NUMBER 8

The tithe should be given into the "storehouse," which today is your local church where you regularly attend and receive your spiritual food and nourishment in order to grow in your Christian life. **Malachi 3:10** is very specific that the whole tithe should be placed into your local church. It is wrong to split up the tithe and give portions into different ministries.

NUMBER 9

Tithing involves worship unto the Lord. A confession of your faith over the tithe declares your redemption from Satan's bondage and a claiming of your tithing benefits. **(Malachi 3:10,11, Deuteronomy 26.)**

NUMBER 10

There are two major rewards that belong to faithful tithers.

1. You release the windows of heaven so that financial blessings come upon yourself.

2. You activate God's rebuke against Satan and the devourer is bound from stealing your finances.

NUMBER 11

From **Malachi 3:10-11** we see that tithing is the only place in the Bible where God challenges the believer to put Him to the test financially. Tithing is the only place in Scripture that God undertakes to rebuke and resist Satan, the thief, for our sakes.

NUMBER 12

Every Christian who isn't honoring the Lord with the tithe is guilty of robbing God, is living under a curse, and will remain in financial bondage until he or she obeys God's Word and begins to tithe. Tithing breaks the curse!

NUMBER 13

Tithing is an acknowledgement that God is the owner

of all and you are only a steward or trustee over your human estate.

NUMBER 14

Tithing is being a good steward. It is acknowledging the Lordship of Jesus in a practical, tangible way.

NUMBER 15

Tithing is declaring that God is our source and that He has blessed and provided for us.

NUMBER 16

We are to be good stewards of the money and resources God has entrusted to us. Tithing is the starting point in our stewardship and the foundation in our giving to God.

NUMBER 17

God should be first in our lives — the tithe is the first-fruits. The tithe is the first tenth — it is the first ten percent of your income. If you give offerings and don't tithe, then you will destroy your harvest because the devourer, the devil, is not rebuked. The ABC's in your giving is your tithe and that should always be the first check you write out as soon as you are paid each week or each month.

NUMBER 18

Giving the tithe acknowledges where your heart is and acknowledges the sovereignty of God.

NUMBER 19

We must realize that tithing didn't begin and end with the law but is an eternal, foundational principle of God's Word.

NUMBER 20

God doesn't ask you to tithe as a punishment. He wants you to tithe so that He can bless you.

NUMBER 21

The tithing Christian will see the hand of the Lord upon his finances. We can never outgive God. Remember, ninety percent of your income with God's blessing is more than one hundred percent without it!

MAKE A COVENANT WITH THE LORD TODAY

It pays to trust and obey God! Let this day be the beginning of a new life of blessing for you. Make a covenant with God, and try Him, as He has said. He has already made a covenant with you and He won't break it.

Bring all the tithes into the storehouse, That there may be food in My house, And prove Me now in this, Says the Lord of hosts, If I will not open for you the windows of heaven and pour you out such blessing, that there will not be room enough to receive it.

Malachi 3:10

Give and it shall be given to you: good measure, pressed down, shaken together, and running over will be put into your bosom. For with the same measure you use, it will be measured back to you.

Luke 6:38

Make this tithing covenant with God today.

"Because the Spirit of the Lord has convinced me that tithing and giving of offerings is Scriptural (according to Malachi 3:8-12) and isn't an optional practice for the obedient Christian, I hereby commit to the Lord that I will be a faithful tither to my local church and a cheerful giver of offerings above the tithe to support anointed ministries in proclaiming the uncompromised Gospel and evangelize the world for Jesus Christ!

"By making this covenant with God, I realize it puts me in a position to receive God's blessings and His protection over my finances, in Jesus' Name!"

Name: _____

Signed: _____

Date: _____

This covenant, earnestly and sincerely made and faithfully kept, will prove to be the key to God's storehouse — the open road to Scriptural financial blessing and success!